BLAZERS

HORSEPOWER

LOWRIDERS

by Matt Doeden

Reading Consultant:

Barbara J. Fox

Reading Specialist

North Carolina State University

Capstone press

Mankato, Minnesota

Blazers is published by Capstone Press,
151 Good Counsel Drive, P.O. Box 669, Mankato, Minnesota 56002.
www.capstonepress.com

Library of Congress Cataloging-in-Publication Data
Doeden, Matt.
    Lowriders / by Matt Doeden.
    p. cm.—(Blazers—horsepower)
    Includes bibliographical references and index.
    ISBN 0-7368-3789-2 (hardcover)
    1. Lowriders—Juvenile literature. I. Title. II. Series.
TL255.2.D64 2005
629.28'72—dc22   2004020810

Summary: Discusses lowriders and their main features.

Editorial Credits
Erika L. Shores, editor; Jason Knudson, set designer; Patrick D.
    Dentinger, book designer; Wanda Winch, photo researcher;
    Scott Thoms, photo editor

Photo Credits
Photo courtesy of Alex Navarro, 6–7
Ron Kimball Stock/Ron Kimball, cover, 10–11, 12, 13, 14, 15, 16–17,
    18–19, 20-21, 22–23, 24–25, 26-27, 28–29
straightclownin/Jose Romero, 4–5, 8–9

1 2 3 4 5 6 10 09 08 07 06 05

TABLE OF CONTENTS

LOWRIDERS

A crowd gathers in a parking lot. A lowrider pulls up. Loud music blasts from the stereo.

Nearby, a car owner uses a
remote control to make a lowrider
dance and hop. The crowd cheers.

Later, people gather for a jumping contest. Judges measure how high the car bounces off the ground.

LOWRIDER DESIGN

Lowriders ride low to the ground. Owners change the suspension systems to get the cars as close to the ground as possible.

Some owners add hydraulic systems. These pumps raise and lower a car. Drivers control the pumps with switches.

Hydraulic system

BLAZER FACT

Some owners use air bags instead of hydraulic systems to raise and lower their lowriders.

Many lowrider owners add
brightly colored rims to the
wheels of their cars.

The 1964 Chevrolet Impala is one of the most common lowrider car models.

Rim

LOWRIDER DIAGRAM

Engine

Steering wheel

Rim

Custom paint

Suspension spring

OUTSIDE DETAILS

Many lowriders have custom paint jobs. Owners paint designs or pictures on their cars.

Some owners add doors that
open backward. Other owners
remove the tops from their lowriders.

BLAZER FACT

Doors that open backward are called suicide doors because they are dangerous to riders during crashes.

Owners want their engines to look good. They add new chrome parts. Some owners paint designs under the hood.

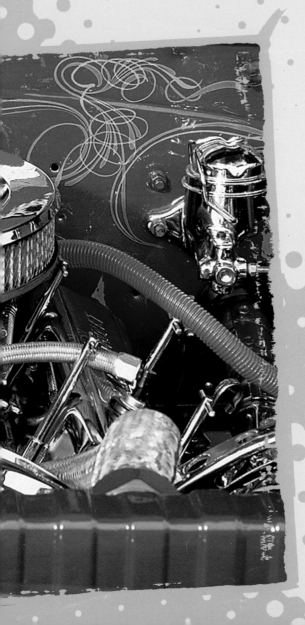

INSIDE DETAILS

Lowrider owners also work on the inside and trunks of their cars. They add sound systems that can be heard from blocks away.

Speaker

Owners cover the inside with
soft fabric. They make their
lowriders unlike any other car.

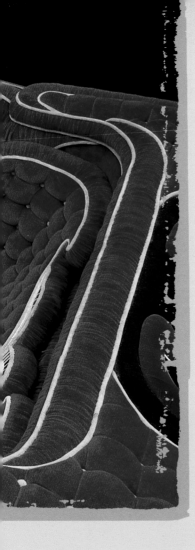

BLAZER FACT

One famous lowrider had an aquarium with fish inside the car.

HYDRAULICS IN ACTION!

GLOSSARY

chrome (KROHM)—a coating of a metallic substance called chromium; chrome gives objects a shiny, metallic appearance.

custom (KUHSS-tuhm)—specially done or made

hydraulic system (hye-DRAW-lik SISS-tuhm)—a system of pumps powered by fluid forced through chambers or pipes; the hydraulic system raises and lowers the car.

rim (RIM)—the outer decorative part of a wheel

suspension system (suh-SPEN-shuhn SISS-tuhm)—the system of springs and shock absorbers that absorbs a car's up-and-down movements

READ MORE

Maurer, Tracy. *Lowriders.* Roaring Rides. Vero Beach, Fla.: Rourke, 2004.

Parr, Danny. *Lowriders.* Race Car Legends. Philadelphia: Chelsea House, 2001.

Parr, Danny. *Lowriders.* Wild Rides! Mankato, Minn.: Capstone Press, 2002.

INTERNET SITES

FactHound offers a safe, fun way to find Internet sites related to this book. All of the sites on FactHound have been researched by our staff.

Here's how:

1. Visit *www.facthound.com*
2. Type in this special code **0736837892** for age-appropriate sites. Or, enter a search word related to this book for a more general search.
3. Click on the **Fetch It** button.

FactHound will fetch the best sites for you!

INDEX